THE BOOK OF CULTS: POP CULTURE POISON

PRESENTED BY:
THE ANTI-CULT ORGANIZATION

The beliefs expressed in this book are those of The Anti-Cult Organization.

If you share these beliefs—or if you're ready to join the deprogramming:

Follow us everywhere: @theanticultorg
Visit: theanticult.org

Copyright © 2025 The Anti-Cult Organization
All rights reserved.
ISBN: 979-8-9989635-0-6

SIDE A

1	**The Cult of the Sitcom**	5
2	**The Cult of the Rom-Com**	10
3	**The Cult of Reality TV**	14
4	**The True Crime Cult.**	18
5	**The Influencer Cult.**	23
6	**The Beyhive & Swifties.**	29
7	**The Wellness Cult.**	35
8	**The Mental Health Cult.**	40
9	**The Self-Care Cult.**	46
10	**The Boss Babe Cult.**	52

SIDE B

1	**The Hustle Cult.**	58
2	**Cult of Retard Rap.**	63
3	**The Indie Cult.**	69
4	**The Cult of Cancel.**	74
5	**The Gamer Church.**	80
6	**The Incel Cult.**	83
7	**The Selfie Religion.**	87
9	**The Cult of the Biopic**	97
10	**The Cult of Nostalgia.**	103

THE CULT OF THE SITCOM

Indoctrination Phrase: *"You'll always have your friends."*
Core Doctrine: *Trauma-bonded roommates = found family*
Truth Bomb: *You weren't watching a show—you were studying a blueprint for performative connection.*

Let's not fuck around—the sitcom wasn't comedy.
It was behavioral training in a laugh track wrapper.

You thought you were bonding with a show,
but you were learning how to contort yourself
into socially acceptable dysfunction.

You were taught:
- Conflict is funny if resolved in 22 minutes.
- Emotional repression is charming if it comes with punchlines.
- "Friendship" means never growing—just rotating neuroses in an open-concept living room.

These weren't characters.
They were templates.

- The neurotic one.
- The sexy one.
- The dumb one.
- The "ethnic" one *(if they made it past the pilot).*

They didn't just model behavior. **They mandated it.**

The vibe of every sitcom friend group?
White, beige, borderline sociopathic.
Sarcasm as intimacy.
Joblessness as quirk.
Emotional constipation as comedic tension.

Their "quirks" weren't personality—**they were performance.**
Market-tested. Focus-group-approved.
People who only existed so you could feel normal for numbing out.

> *"It's okay to be deeply broken—as long as you're charming about it."*

You know what a laugh track really is?
A fucking obedience bell.

It trains you to respond to emotional confusion with social approval.

– Don't know how to feel? Don't worry, we'll tell you when it's funny.
– Can't process awkward silence? Here's a studio giggle to numb the tension.

It's not just annoying. **It's conditioning.**
A psychological cattle prod that says:
"Don't think—just react."

The genre romanticized the idea that you don't need therapy.
You just need brunch.

– Someone dies? Joke about it.
– Someone's toxic? *Eh, that's just Chandler.*
– Someone shows growth? Sabotage the arc to preserve the dynamic.

Because healing doesn't test well.
The sitcom formula required stasis.

Any sign of character evolution threatened the core illusion: that your dysfunction is endearing as long as it's predictable.

For decades, "diversity" meant throwing in a Black friend three seasons deep
with no backstory and no agency.

– Latino? If they're hot and heavily accented.
– Asian? Rare.
– Gay? A punchline first, a person second.
– Neurodivergent? *Please. This isn't a horror film.*

It wasn't just about who was on screen.
It was about **what types of pain were allowed to exist.**

 – **White middle-class dysfunction?** Prime time.
 – **Generational trauma or systemic oppression?**
Too "serious." Doesn't pair well with theme songs and canned laughter.

The Cult of the Sitcom gave us the idea that:
Proximity = intimacy.
Banter = belonging.
If you just hang out enough, trauma will evolve into inside jokes.

But here's the truth:
Most people don't have "ride or die" friend groups.
They have **anxiety-fueled group chats** full of people they're afraid to outgrow.

And if you grew up feeling othered, isolated, weird, or wrong—
these shows didn't make you feel seen.
They made you feel broken for not fitting in.

You didn't grow up on sitcoms.
You were socialized by them.

You absorbed scripts that told you:
 – Real feelings are too heavy.
 – Seriousness is unattractive.
 – Being the punchline is a path to love.

And you wonder why:
 – You apologize before crying?
 – You crack jokes mid-breakdown?
 – You can't tell if your friendships are real or just trauma choreography?

You weren't laughing with them.
You were rehearsing your own repression.

The Cult of the Sitcom didn't teach you friendship.
It taught you performance.

It didn't teach you love.
It taught you loyalty to dysfunction.

And if you're still clinging to those reruns like they raised you?
They did.
And that's the fucking problem.

THE CULT OF THE ROM-COM

Indoctrination Phrase: *"He was just scared of his feelings."*
Core Doctrine: *Emotional terrorism = foreplay*
Truth Bomb: *You weren't watching a love story. You were watching a woman negotiate with red flags for 97 minutes.*

Rom-coms weren't about romance.
They were about **repackaging psychological warfare as compatibility.**

The premise?

- Meet someone who's completely wrong for you.
- Ignore your gut.
- Sacrifice your dignity.

And eventually? They'll change—but only after you suffer enough to earn it.

That wasn't a plot.
That was a trauma bond in high-definition.

The "bad boy with a heart of gold" wasn't misunderstood.
He was emotionally unavailable, verbally abusive, and allergic to accountability.

But the movie taught you:
 – If you're charming enough…
 – If you're patient enough…
 – If you're lovable enough…
He'll finally text you back.

That's not love.
That's conditioning.

You were sold the idea that **being chosen is the goal.**
But the process of getting chosen?
Ritualized self-abandonment.

 – He's rude to you in Act I? He's probably your soulmate.
 – He ignores you at the party? He's struggling with vulnerability.
 – He gaslights you about your own instincts? Don't worry—he'll apologize in the rain.

Rom-coms taught you to wait for transformation.
That if you suffered enough in silence, a man would be reborn in your image.

Cue the orchestral swell.
Cue the running-through-an-airport scene.
Cue the delusion.

They made **codependence cinematic.**

And women in these films?
Always hyper-competent, high-achieving, emotionally literate—
and yet somehow desperate for the approval of a man who hasn't done a single fucking thing to deserve her attention.

She doesn't have time for herself.
She has time for his potential.

Potential isn't love.
It's unpaid labor.

The rom-com formula wasn't just fiction.
It was **emotional choreography.**

It taught you to:
- ✖ Ignore your intuition
- ✖ Accept inconsistency as mystery
- ✖ Translate neglect as charm
- ✖ Believe that settling is strength

And the "funny best friend"?
Always the truth-teller. Always on the sidelines.
Because women with clarity don't get love interests—**they get comic relief roles.**

You were trained to prioritize the fantasy over the facts.
To believe that love is a conquest.
That **chemistry = chaos.**
That **boundaries are plot holes.**

This genre didn't just mislead you.
It rewired you.

It told you you were "too picky" if you didn't want to be treated like shit.
It told you that having standards meant you'd end up alone.
It told you that fighting all the time meant "passion."
That **manipulation was masculinity.**
That the more you struggled, the more "real" it was.

They called it love.
It was behavioral exposure therapy.

You're not bitter.
You're deprogramming.

You're not unromantic.
You just finally realized that "grand gesture" was a distraction from **chronic disrespect.**

So if you've been sitting there wondering why:
 – You confuse anxiety with butterflies
 – You mistake silence for mystery
 – You stay in cycles longer than your intuition tells you to

It's not a flaw.
It's a fucking feature.

The Cult of the Rom-Com didn't show you love.
It showed you how to justify its absence.

And if you still think
"they'll change if I love them enough"?
You're not in love.
You're in a hostage negotiation with your own self-worth.

THE CULT OF REALITY TV

Indoctrination Phrase: *"I'm not here to make friends."*
Core Doctrine: *Manufactured chaos = authenticity*
Truth Bomb: *You weren't watching "real life." You were mainlining dysfunction edited for consumption.*

Let's get this straight:
Reality TV is not real.

It's a trauma theme park with confessional booths.
A circus of broken people baited into acting worse for rent money and screen time.

You think you're "observing."
You're not.
You're complicit.

You're watching humanity as spectacle, and calling it personality.

And what are they always competing for?

✔ A rose
✔ A marriage
✔ A job in a toxic workplace
✔ The approval of a millionaire who calls themselves a "coach" but acts like a cult leader with a tanning bed addiction

It's all the same show.
Just new branding.
Humiliation for hire.

The format?

- Start with 12 people.
- Isolate them. Starve them emotionally.
- Cut the cameras to make them question reality.
- Add alcohol.
- Roll tape.

Someone cries = content.
Someone snaps = storyline.
Someone gets exploited = *"fan favorite."*

What you're watching isn't resilience.
It's a fucking breakdown curated for brand partnerships.

And don't get it twisted—these aren't "bad people."
They're people dropped into a social experiment with no consent and one rule:

Be unforgettable or be deleted.

Conflict is currency.
Emotional damage = influencer deals.

Get enough screen time, and **your trauma becomes your career.**

But the cult doesn't just live on set.
It lives in the audience.

You, rooting for the villain because they're "iconic."
You, tearing down the one woman who sets a boundary.
You, convinced that chaos = charisma.

This isn't entertainment.
It's mass gaslighting.

You're being trained to:
— Crave conflict
— Confuse toxicity with confidence
— Accept surveillance as connection
— Believe that emotional volatility = truth

Because when real life feels flat, what do you do?

Turn on the TV and mainline drama until your nervous system can't tell the difference.

The line between watching a breakdown and becoming one gets thinner every season.

And the worst part?

You think you're better than them.

That's the final indoctrination.

You think you're above it.
You laugh. You judge. You tweet.

But if you've ever:
– Fought for attention
– Performed your pain
– Been in a group that punished you for healing
– Told a half-truth because it made you more likable

**Congratulations.
You've played the game.**

The cameras just weren't on.

Reality TV isn't a guilty pleasure.
It's a collective confession booth.

And we're all in the background, nodding along, asking,
"Who's getting voted off the island next?"
As if we're not the ones **building the island.**

THE TRUE CRIME CULT

Indoctrination Phrase: *"I'm just into psychology."*
Core Doctrine: *Other people's trauma = quirky hobby*
Truth Bomb: *You're not investigating justice. You're fetishizing fear in 1.5x playback speed.*

Let's be clear:
This isn't about justice.
This is about **entertainment through exploitation.**

You're not "fascinated by the mind of a killer."
You're **addicted to the sound of a woman screaming** and calling it "self care."

Murder podcasts to fall asleep?
That's not curiosity.
That's conditioning.

And the playlist is soaked in blood.
The True Crime Cult loves a victim—but only the right kind.

- White.
- Blonde.
- Photogenic.
- Murdered, but not messy.
- Missing, but not complicated.

Because the minute a victim is:
– Black
– Trans
– Sex-working
– Disabled
– Undocumented
– Or otherwise inconvenient?

The plot gets dropped.
The "audience" isn't invested.
The algorithm isn't generous.

These aren't stories. **They're sacrifices.**
Bodies turned into content.
Families turned into footnotes.

You get a two-part episode.
They get a lifetime of grief.

And don't come in here with *"but it raises awareness."*
No, it doesn't.
It raises **engagement**.

And sells tote bags that say *"stay sexy, don't get murdered"* while you sip from your *"stabby vibes"* tumbler.

This isn't activism.
This is trauma cosplay.

And the hosts?

Soft-spoken, wine-drunk narrators
weaving tragedy into bedtime stories.

> "Hi friends, today's episode is about a triple homicide.
> But first, let me tell you about this new mattress I've been loving."

What the fuck are we doing.

You're not woke for consuming true crime.
You're **sedated.**

You've been spoon-fed violence until:
 – You confuse fear with awareness
 – You think your "interest" makes you informed
 – You can recall Bundy's shoe size
but not the name of the girl he killed behind a dumpster

You're being trained to:
 — See horror as bingeable
 — See pain as palatable

 — See death as digestible
if it's delivered with pastel fonts and gentle narration

And if that doesn't disturb you?
That's the cult at work.

Because what started as curiosity
becomes identity.

You wear *"true crime addict"* like a badge.
You say, *"I could never kill someone... but I know how to hide a body."*

You think it's a joke.
But **you're swimming in the punchline.**

Here's the thing:
The real monsters aren't the ones in the stories.

They're:
 – The networks that mass-produce suffering as serialized entertainment
 – The fans who demand sequels before bodies are buried
 – The streaming platforms that renew trauma like it's a sitcom

But no one wants to hear that.

Because it's easier to dissect a killer's brain
than look at your own reflection.
Easier to judge a murderer
than examine your own numbness.

Easier to say *"this is educational"*
than admit you're entertained.

So keep listening.
Keep nodding along as another girl disappears,
another mother cries,
another town gets shattered for ratings.

Just don't pretend you're innocent.

The True Crime Cult didn't make you evil.
It made you comfortable.

Comfortable enough to treat someone's last breath like background noise while you fold laundry.

And if that doesn't haunt you?
That's exactly how the cult survives.

THE INFLUENCER CULT

Indoctrination Phrase: *"Just be yourself."*
Core Doctrine: *Authenticity is an aesthetic*
Truth Bomb: *You're not following them. You're funding your own manipulation.*

Let's stop pretending influencers are "relatable."
They're not relatable.
They're algorithmically engineered parasites
with ring lights and identity theft issues.

You think you're watching someone live their life.
You're watching someone monetize yours.

Their brand isn't them.
It's the version of you they think you'll envy enough to fund.

Here's the formula:

1. Manufacture intimacy
2. Weaponize vulnerability
3. Sell you the solution to a problem they created on purpose

Because what is a *"raw"* post if not a strategically ugly cry sponsored by a journaling app?

What is a *"real moment"* if not a curated breakdown edited between Adderall and affiliate links?

They're not sharing.
They're farming.

– Mining your trauma for comments
– Mining your insecurities for likes
– Mining your "omg same" for sales conversions

And the worst part?

You think it's empowering.
You think "seeing someone be vulnerable" means they're safe.
You think someone calling it *content* makes it real.

But if it's monetized?
It's not confession—it's commerce.

And the content cycles?

God help us.

- *Hot girl walks*
- *De-influencing videos* that still include links
- *Mental health check-ins* that end with a 10% off code
- *Trauma stories* shared with full glam and TikTok transitions

We're watching people **brand their breakdowns in real time** and calling it "community."

No.
This isn't vulnerability.
This is emotional strip-mining.

This is neoliberal loneliness as performance art.

They didn't "just build a platform."
They built a cult with comment sections—

– where they're both savior and victim
– where dissent is deleted
– where concern is called "jealousy"
– where their trauma is monetized
– and yours is crowdsourced

And let's talk about the goddamn filters.

- Face filters
- Thought filters
- Language filters

Every word is beta-tested.
Every caption emotionally sterilized.
Every photo screams *"Look how real I am"* while bathing in twenty minutes of Facetune.

But hey, it's okay—because **they're just being "authentic," right?**

Let me ask you something:

 – Would you still follow them if they didn't look like you wished you looked?
 – Would you still "relate" if they weren't palatable enough for the algorithm?
 – Would you still take their advice if it didn't come with a discount code?

You're not connecting.
You're consuming.

You're not being seen.
You're being sold a simulation of being seen.

Because this cult thrives on one thing:
Making you believe that you're broken—and that they can fix you for $29.99.

They'll tell you to *stop comparing*—
while feeding you an image designed to be aspirational.

They'll say *"healing isn't linear"*—
right before uploading a Reel about how breathwork saved their marriage.

They'll tell you *"you're enough"*—
right before selling you another version of who you should be.

And if you try to call it out?

- You're a hater
- You don't "get it"
- You're "projecting"
- You're "toxic"
- You're "not supporting women"

Nah.
What you're not doing is drinking the green juice-flavored Kool-Aid.

So let's be honest:

The Influencer Cult isn't just toxic.
It's industrialized codependency.

It's the digital co-opting of every self-love movement that ever meant something.
It's cult-leadership as a content strategy.

They're not helping you grow.
They're teaching you to narrate your own breakdown for clout.

They're not building a brand.
They're building a platform-shaped panopticon
and convincing you that visibility is safety.

But guess what?

If your worth only exists when it's being witnessed—
You're not free.
You're trapped in the feed.

So the next time you watch someone cry on camera and call it content,
ask yourself: Who profits from my empathy today?

THE BEYHIVE & THE SWIFTIES

Indoctrination Phrase: *"You just don't understand her power."*
Core Doctrine: *Pop devotion = moral superiority*
Truth Bomb: *You're not a fan. You're a disciple—and you tithe in streams and blind loyalty.*

Let's start with Beyoncé.
Because this isn't just celebrity worship.
This is **organized spiritual warfare** with glitter and goat's blood.

And no, that's not a metaphor.
She is literally a witch.
Like, for real.

The rituals.
The symbols.
The lineage.
The hex rumors.
The high priestess energy cloaked in Balmain.

There are receipts.

This is a woman whose stage performances contain more sigils than a Wiccan handbook.
She's not dancing—**she's summoning.**

And you?
You're channeling her power unknowingly while screaming *"SLAY QUEEN"* with tears running down your face.

You think you're vibing.
You're actually being spiritually initiated.

And look—this is not slander.
It's respect.

Beyoncé isn't fake.
She's terrifyingly real.
She doesn't sell music.
She transmits energy.

She's the only person alive who could drop a three-hour album about horse riding and marital trauma—
and somehow it's a religious experience.

But that's what makes the Beyhive a true cult.

Because it's not about the art.

It's about the unquestioned divinity of the source.

You are not allowed to critique her.
You are not allowed to question her.

You are not even allowed to joke—
unless it's about how *"people who don't get it just aren't spiritually evolved yet."*

The Beyhive doesn't defend her.
They enforce her.

It's one thing to be talented.
It's another to be the **high priestess of Black capitalist feminism, gender-coded spiritual warfare, and aesthetic perfectionism—all at once.**

She dropped *Lemonade* and women started re-evaluating their marriages.
She dropped *Black Is King* and everyone became a part-time Egyptologist overnight.

She breathes and the internet resets itself.

Her fans will drag your family, your ancestors, your unborn children—
just for misquoting a lyric.

But maybe that's the point.
Beyoncé doesn't ask for worship. She demands alignment.

You're not in a fandom.
You're in a devotional practice.

And if she *is* a witch (and again, she is)—

then worshipping her isn't even your fault.

You didn't fall for a pop star.
You were hexed through harmonics and choreography.

So let's move on to Taylor Swift.
Different cult.
Same spell.

But instead of blood magic and protection candles,
the Swifties believe in something even more dangerous:
hope.

This is a fandom powered entirely by people who still believe in love.

Not healthy love.
Not grounded love.

But that delusional, music-box, coded-in-tears,
"maybe he'll come back if I cry on the piano" kind of love.

These are not just songs.
They're **emotional vision boards** for people who think their high school breakup was soul contract shit.

You know how powerful you have to be to make adults cry over scarf metaphors?

You know how brainwashed someone has to be to believe that a pop star with 500 breakups *just hasn't found the right one yet*?

The Swiftie cult is the most terrifying kind—
because they believe she's healing them.

- One lyric at a time
- One re-recorded album at a time
- One vaguely queer-coded easter egg at a time

(But only just enough to keep the gay fans hopeful without ever confirming anything.
See? That's cult-level manipulation.)

Taylor is the **benevolent girl-god for the emotionally malnourished.**

The patron saint of:
- Crying into throw pillows
- Texting your ex at 2AM
- Romanticizing narcissistic abuse
- Believing you're *"the problem"* in a cute way

This isn't fandom.
This is codependency with a chorus.

And when you try to opt out?
Good fucking luck.

Every wedding, every coffee shop, every TikTok is a shrine to her melancholy.
You can't escape her.
You just get absorbed.

So whether you're lighting intention candles to *Cuff It*

or analyzing 10-minute breakdowns like sacred scripture...

Know this:
You're not listening to music.
You're surrendering to ritual.

The Beyhive & Swifties don't just worship.
They convert.

And the worst part?
You might not even realize you've joined.

Because in these cults,
the spell is disguised as the soundtrack to your healing.

THE WELLNESS CULT

Indoctrination Phrase: *"Your body keeps the score."*
Core Doctrine: *If you're not healed, you're not trying hard enough.*
Truth Bomb: *You didn't buy peace—you bought aesthetic self-flagellation with an invoice from Shopify.*

Welcome to the Church of Wellness,
where the sins are trauma,
the tithe is $4,999 retreats,
and salvation is sold in seasonal drops.

This cult doesn't wear robes.
It wears Lululemon Align pants and a quartz-infused Stanley cup.

It doesn't chant in Latin.
It chants in hashtags:

#healing
#selflove
#nervoussystemreset
#somaticsovereignty

But don't get it twisted—**this isn't spirituality.**
This is performative enlightenment rebranded as subscription-based self-regulation.

They will sell you:
- Breathwork packages
- Trauma release bootcamps
- Chakra alignment crystals
- Guided DMT ceremonies in Bali led by a DJ named Forest
- Ayahuasca journeys where Karen finds her "divine feminine" and then vomits on a shaman's rug for 30K

They'll call it sacred.
But it's just colonialism with better lighting.

You are not healing.
You are consuming the illusion of healing.

And the worse you feel, the more you spend.
That's not progress.
That's a feedback loop of profitable self-doubt.

Feeling anxious? Buy magnesium.
Feeling tired? Buy mushrooms.
Feeling disconnected?

Get on a plane, find an "indigenous" retreat,
and treat their sacred medicine like your personal upgrade from therapy.

Because nothing says alignment like **trauma tourism.**

These retreats don't change lives.
They just photograph well.

Curated disassociations with:
 – Sunrise yoga
 – Vegan bowls
 – The same five white women fake-crying during a cacao ceremony
 – Posting *"my heart cracked open today 🌙 👁️ ✨"*

The Wellness Cult doesn't care if you get better.
It cares if you get repeatable.

Because when your suffering becomes your personal brand,
your *"healing journey"* becomes a fucking marketing funnel.

You are now a customer of your own emotional instability.

But don't worry—they've got everything you need:

 – Guided somatic workshops from a woman who got "certified" in a two-week Zoom
 – An "ancestral" trauma course taught by a girl named Kelsey who's never met her grandparents

- EFT tapping
- Inner child reparenting
- Shadow work
- Nervous system hacking
- "Fuck the patriarchy" yoga flows

It's all there.
Curated. Marketed. Monetized.
Healing rebranded as hustle.

And if you ever stop to question it?

They'll say:
- You're "resisting"
- Your ego is flaring up
- You "don't want to do the work"

Translation: You're interfering with the sale.

The Wellness Cult doesn't tolerate doubt.
Doubt doesn't convert.

So you keep:
- Meditating on problems that aren't yours
- Taking ownership of wounds you didn't create
- Blaming your nervous system for living in a world that is actively traumatizing you

---

Because God forbid anyone say the real shit:

Maybe you're not broken.
Maybe the world is.

And maybe
you can't breathwork your way out of late-stage capitalism.

But that doesn't sell tickets.

So instead, we chant:
"I am healing."
"I am aligned."
"I am open."

Meanwhile:
- Your credit card is crying
- Your boundaries are disintegrating
- Your therapist just started offering moon circle reiki

This isn't freedom.
This is spiritual bypassing in a $98 float tank.

The Cult of Wellness didn't save you.
It just gave you something prettier to be trapped in.

So next time someone tells you *"healing isn't linear,"* ask them:

**Is your healing nonlinear...
or just on autopay?**

THE MENTAL HEALTH CULT

Indoctrination Phrase: *"Normalize everything."*
Core Doctrine: *Pathology is personality*
Truth Bomb: *They made your pain a punchline, your diagnosis a trend, and your vulnerability a business model.*

Welcome to the Mental Healt Cult,
where trauma is branding,
ADHD is merch,
and therapy is a personality quiz with pastel aesthetics.

You're not healing.
You're being marketed to.

By people who told you for decades that being "broken" made you dangerous—
then rebranded your survival as quirky when it became profitable.

Let's rewind:

- First, they demonized it.
- Medicated it.
- Mocked it.
- Institutionalized it.
- Weaponized it against you.

Then—after enough early adopters bled in public—they packaged your pathology as self-discovery.

> "Oh you stim? Same lol."
> "Oh you dissociate? I do that too when I'm bored in meetings."
> "Oh you have ADHD? Me too. I can't focus on boring stuff either."

NO.
You don't "relate."
You're commodifying the symptoms of people who had to crawl through systems that hated them for existing.

Fake ASMR?
That's a fucking symptom simulator.

It's not soothing.
It's mimicking neurodivergence for clicks.
You're not creating calm.
You're cosplaying regulation.

And ADHD?
It's become the **punchline of the internet.**

Your executive dysfunction.
Your chronic overwhelm.
Your memory lapses.
Your nervous system screaming in every room—

Now they're **content pillars.**

You're not misunderstood.
You're just the main character in someone else's brand strategy.

They turned our lived reality into meme templates.
Not for awareness.
But for relatability.

So they could own the conversation
and drown out the people who actually live this shit.

And then it gets darker.

What happens when people start talking about autism?

Suddenly:
 – We get whispers of eugenics
 – The conversation gets hijacked by alt-right creeps
 – Neurodivergence becomes associated with genius, detachment, and... Nazi ideology

You think I'm exaggerating?

Go look.
Reddit threads.
Incel forums.
Dog whistles dressed in diagnostic language.

They're trying to build a new class of **"selectively superior outcasts."**

Not to help autistic people—
To weaponize the label and avoid accountability.

So now we've got:
Therapized fascism in cute little outfits.
Hyper-analyzed childhoods.
"Shadow work" as a power play.
Influencers monetizing trauma from the safety of ring lights and email funnels.

And what's the aesthetic right now?

Everyone's emo again.

But not in a revolutionary way.
Not in a "burn it all down" way.

Now it's:

> "I'm in my healing era."
> "I'm sad but slaying."
> "Vulnerable baddie."
> "I'm not okay and that's okay... please subscribe."

You think that's progress?

That's the final stage of indoctrination:

- Turn your resistance into a niche
- Turn your emotions into performance
- Turn your crisis into content

This wasn't healing.
This was cultural grooming.

- Slow-burn conditioning
- Demonize therapy until the masses fear it
- Gaslight early adopters into shame and self-doubt
- Then flip it into a brand
- And punish those same early adopters for being "too negative," "too intense," or "not aesthetic enough" for the healing space they built

That's America.
That's capitalism.
That's the fucking cult playbook.

They teach you to hate yourself.
Then they sell you a version of yourself that's more palatable.
More monetizable.
More aligned with the brand of someone who never lived it but knows how to sell it.

So no—your openness isn't freedom.
It's formatted.

Your trauma isn't sacred.
It's licensed.

Your vulnerability isn't yours anymore.
It's user-generated content.

The Mental Health Cult didn't teach you to heal.
It taught you to package your pain like a product and hope the algorithm likes it.

THE SELF-CARE CULT

Indoctrination Phrase: *"You can't pour from an empty cup."*
Core Doctrine: *Burnout is a branding opportunity*
Truth Bomb: *If it comes with a product tag, it's not self-care. It's lifestyle laundering.*

We need to talk about the fact that there is even a "self-care" section:

- In stores
- On websites
- On TikTok
- In your damn planner

Do you hear how fucking dystopian that is?

We live in a world so emotionally barren, so systemically hostile, so soul-drainingly exploitative—
that we had to invent a category to remind people to breathe.
To rest.
To drink water.

And then we had the audacity to monetize it.

You're not practicing self-care.
You're buying back your humanity.

And even then—**only if you can afford the entry fee.**

- Aromatherapy
- Digital detox kits
- Weighted blankets
- Subscription boxes
- Guided journaling packs
- Dry brushing kits for $89
- "Self-soothing bundles" from women named Rachel who wear flowy pants and talk like they're floating

This isn't healing.
This is emotional gentrification.

"Self-care" didn't used to be a category.
It used to be survival.

A moment to hold yourself
before the world tried to break you again.

– A stolen breath
– A hot meal
– A fucking nap

Now?

Now it's an aesthetic.
A vibe.
A curated flatlay of lavender candles and handwritten mantras scribbled in pens you were upsold during a "healing workshop."

This cult taught you that **being okay requires accessories.**

And if you're not "rejuvenated" after:

- A skincare routine
- A silent retreat
- 15 minutes of intentional breathwork

Well, clearly you're just doing it wrong.

Because the system didn't just strip you of rest.
It repackaged it into something you had to earn.

Now rest is a reward.
Not a right.

And "boundaries"?
Just another concept to fail at.

– You say no and feel guilty
– You rest and feel lazy
– You pause and feel behind

So what do you do?

– You book the fucking spa day
– You buy the journal
– You download the meditation app that secretly tracks your data and sells it to an insurance provider

Because they've convinced you that burnout is your fault.
That your exhaustion is personal, not systemic.
That your inability to function is a branding issue.

So now you light a candle and call it resistance.
You unplug for a day and post about it on Instagram.
You drink tea and say *"I'm reclaiming my time"*
while capitalism counts your breaths and bills you for them.

You are **being soothed into silence.**

Because here's the truth:

- If self-care doesn't include dismantling the systems that broke you in the first place,
  It's not care. It's compliance.

- If your rest doesn't disrupt your productivity cycle,
  It's not healing. It's optimization.

- If your boundary-setting is just a way to be better at work tomorrow,
  You're not protecting your peace. You're polishing your cage.

The Self-Care Cult told you to love yourself—
but only in ways that could be monetized, aestheticized, and easily added to your cart.

And if you're not glowing, centered, and emotionally fluent after:

- Three soy wax candles
- A $120 "healing crystal"

Guess who they'll blame?

You.

Not the job that's draining you.
Not the childhood that shaped you.
Not the patriarchy that gaslit you into believing exhaustion is empowerment.

You.

Because this cult isn't here to heal you.
It's here to make your symptoms marketable.

And if you ever stop buying?

- You're not "doing the work"
- You're "regressing"
- You're "not prioritizing yourself"
- You're "out of alignment"

Fuck that.

You don't need a "ritual."
You need a nap.
You need protection.
You need revolution.

Self-care was never supposed to be a purchase.
It was supposed to be a protest.

But that doesn't sell.
So they made it cute.
They made it pink.
They made it profitable.
And they made it powerless.

THE BOSS BABE CULT

Indoctrination Phrase: *"You have the same 24 hours as Beyoncé."*
Core Doctrine: *Audacity + Canva = Authority*
Truth Bomb: *You're not being empowered. You're being gaslit into a pyramid scheme with better branding.*

Let's go straight for the throat.

The Boss Babe Cult isn't about business.
It's about delusion marketed as destiny.

This is the cult of fake empowerment, built on:

– Buzzwords
– Bronzer
– Borderline MLM theology

Where "belief in yourself" is the product,
and **shame is the marketing funnel.**

Because let's be honest:
You've seen these girls.

– 25 years old
– Watched three mindset videos
– Took an "abundance" course from a girl named Kylee who lives in Tulum
– Made $1,200 off a dropshipped water bottle with "queen" in cursive

And now?

– They're a life coach
– Or a business mentor
– Or an *energetic wealth activation strategist* (whatever the fuck that means)

And they'll tell you, with full delusional conviction:

> "I turned my passion into profit."
> "I built a six-figure business in six months."
> "You can too. Just do what I did."

Except what they did was **sell you the idea of success**
while praying you don't ask for receipts.

They're not leaders.
They're up-lines.

They don't sell solutions.
They sell replication.

Do what I did.
Say what I say.
Use my template.
Charge my rates.
Fake my confidence.
Mirror my madness.

It's pyramid hustle disguised as purpose.

The formula?

> "I believed in myself."
> "I aligned my frequency."
> "Now I help women like you."

…Which means they make money **telling other women how to make money by telling other women how to make money.**

That's not coaching.
That's cognitive laundering.

And the bait?

They tell you your way is the wrong way.

- Still working a 9-5? You're stuck in "lack mentality."
- Struggling with motivation? You're "not embodied."
- Questioning their advice? You're "not coachable."

**Translation: If their bullshit doesn't work for you,
you're the problem.**

And it gets worse.

Because they brand their dysfunction as wisdom:

- ✘ Unhealed trauma? "Shadow work queen"
- ✘ Financial illiteracy? "Taking intuitive risks"
- ✘ Zero experience? "I trust my divine downloads"
- ✘ Coercion? "Aligned persuasion"
- ✘ Manipulation? "High-ticket energetics"

They're not guiding you to success.
They're indoctrinating you into complicity.

And if you ever stop and say,
"Wait, isn't this kind of... predatory?"

They'll say:

> "You just don't believe in yourself enough."
> "You're afraid of success."
> "You're playing small."
> "You're not ready for abundance."

Nah, bitch.
I'm just not dumb enough to call debt empowerment.

The Boss Babe Cult isn't female empowerment.
It's feminized capitalism.

It's "girl power" neutered, Botoxed, and packaged with a vision board.
It's financial gaslighting dressed up in gold jewelry and manifestation mantras.

And for the record—
having audacity does not make you wise.

Believing in yourself is cute.
But if your entire career is built on selling belief...

Then what the fuck are you actually doing?

You're trapping other women in the same illusion
you needed to justify your own survival.

You didn't build a business.
You built a funnel
of projection, shame, and spiritual MLM vibes—

Where healing, growth, and worth
are measured in payment plans.

They told you:

– If you didn't buy in, you were "settling"
– If you didn't quit your job, raise your prices, and believe you were already a millionaire
You were "blocking your blessings"

But the real block?
Is them.

These aren't leaders.
They're emotional predators with pretty templates and god complexes.

They sell a **false sense of purpose.**
They manufacture urgency.
They sell "freedom" with a conversion rate.

And the worst part?
They get away with it by calling it sisterhood.

This isn't "women supporting women."
It's women monetizing your wounds.

So next time someone tells you:

> "You just have to trust the process"

Ask them:

- **Whose process?**
- **Who profits?**
- **And what happens if I opt out?**

Because here's the truth:

The Boss Babe Cult didn't teach you to lead.
It taught you to perform success so convincingly you'd forget you were still broke, anxious, and afraid to ask real questions.

THE HUSTLE CULT

Indoctrination Phrase: *"Rise and grind."*
Core Doctrine: *Sleep is weakness. Suffering is sexy. Burnout is a badge.*
Truth Bomb: *You're not building a legacy. You're just slowly dying in high-definition.*

Let's talk about the 5AM psychos.
The "no excuses" bros.
The "cold plunge, creatine, 2-hour gym, 12-hour grind, kale for dinner, four-hour sleep, repeat" brigade.

The Hustle Cult isn't a work ethic.
It's an aesthetic of suffering repackaged as masculinity.

- A performance of exhaustion
- A fetish for burnout
- An emotional eating disorder for achievement

And their god?
Gary Fucking Vee.

The human Red Bull.
The patron saint of yelling at minimum wage workers to start a flipping business on their lunch break.
The guy who turned capitalist psychosis into a motivational Instagram quote carousel.

> "Work 18 hours a day if you love it."
> "Sleep is for people who don't want it bad enough."
> "Don't complain—GRIND."

That's not motivation.
That's a cult leader with a Wi-Fi connection.

These dudes treat self-worth like a spreadsheet.
Every second must be monetized.
Every hour must be optimized.
Every breath must be dedicated to the grind.

Never mind if you're in pain.
Never mind if you're falling apart.
Never mind if your body's screaming.

Pain?
That's a **mindset problem.**

- Feeling tired? You're not passionate enough.
- Feeling overwhelmed? You need to focus harder.
- Want to take a break? You clearly don't want success.

And then they wonder why they're 28 with:

– A podcast
– A protein shake
– **No capacity for human intimacy**

These are the same men who idolize Steve Jobs and Elon Musk
and forget that both built empires on the backs of other people's labor.

You're not a visionary.
You're a glorified task rabbit with delusions of grandeur.

Let's be clear:
Hustle Culture doesn't reward hard work.
It rewards performative obsession.

If you're not suffering publicly,
you're not committed enough.

Because you're not supposed to rest.
You're supposed to weaponize your exhaustion as proof of your moral superiority.

> "I'm tired, therefore I matter."
> "I'm booked, therefore I'm valuable."
>
> "I'm too busy to feel anything, therefore I'm winning."

It's cult math.
And the result?

- ✖ Sleep-deprived zombies
- ✖ Caffeine addictions disguised as productivity
- ✖ Digestive trauma from eating in meetings
- ✖ "Motivational" YouTube videos at 2am while crying into your laptop
- ✖ Therapy avoidance masked as "focus"

You're not building a business.
You're offering your soul to the algorithm in exchange for dopamine crumbs.

They told you "no days off."
But **you were never on to begin with.**

You were just overstimulated and undernourished.
 – Confusing momentum for direction
 – Confusing noise for meaning
 – Confusing motion for purpose

And the cult LOVES that.

Because as long as you keep grinding,
you'll never stop to ask:

 – Who am I actually building this for?
 – What does success even mean to me?
 – Why do I need to suffer to feel worthy?

And if you do stop?
If you do ask?
They'll call you lazy.
Or entitled.
Or soft.

Because the greatest threat to the Hustle Cult
is a man who doesn't need productivity to prove his worth.

Let's be real:

– You're not going to grind your way out of generational trauma
– You're not going to optimize your nervous system with a Google Calendar and a gallon of water
– You're not going to cold shower your way into inner peace

You're just going to burn out.

And when you do?

They won't help you.
They'll replace you.

The Hustle Cult doesn't care who you are.
It cares what you produce.

And when you can't anymore?
There's a new 5AM bro ready to scream into a ring light and tell the next generation to *"just want it more."*

So fuck the grind.
Fuck Gary Vee.
Fuck the LinkedIn martyrs and the burnout evangelists.

You don't need to hustle harder.
You need to wake the fuck up.

THE CULT OF RETARD RAP

Indoctrination Phrase: *"It's just a vibe."*
Core Doctrine: *Dumbing down is safer than waking up.*
Truth Bomb: *You're not vibing. You're being systemically sedated with designer beats and lobotomized lyrics.*

Let's cut the beat.

You ever wonder why the real ones disappeared? Why nobody's platforming the artists who say something that might make you think instead of just making your ass move?

It's not a coincidence.
It's a takedown.

A strategic, slow-drip euthanizing of thought rap—
because the minute hip-hop stopped being "ghetto" and started becoming educational,
the system went DEFCON 1.

Because guess what happened when Nas,
Public Enemy, Dead Prez, early Kendrick, Lupe, Mos Def, Talib, early Common,
even fucking Pac—
started putting consciousness into the beat?

White suburban kids started listening.
They started learning.

 – About redlining
 – About mass incarceration
 – About COINTELPRO
 – About how this country has always thrived off Black bodies, broken families, and buried truths

That's when alarm bells went off.

How do you stop the spread of revolutionary education disguised as entertainment?

Easy.
You don't shut it down.
You flood the market with noise.

Welcome to **Retard Rap**—the industry's perfect poison.

✔ The beat
✔ The bass
✔ The bounce
✔ The feeling

But no fucking content.

– Mumbling
– Repetition
– Hooks on a loop
– Lyrics about money, pussy, and murder
with no context, no message, no roots

Just dopamine and dissociation on shuffle.

Because when you can't silence a people,
you saturate them.

– Control the frequency
– Manipulate the mood
– Erase the message

You give the illusion of expression—
but only within controlled parameters.
Only if it doesn't disrupt the system.
Only if it doesn't inspire consciousness.

That's why inflammatory is allowed, but informative is not.
They'll give a deal to every codeine-soaked autotune goblin
who'll chant about killing his own people for a check—
but God forbid someone gets on the mic and says the system is the real enemy.

That gets you shadowbanned.
That gets you called "angry," "too deep," "not commercial."

That gets your deal pulled.
Because "ghetto" music isn't a threat
until it wakes the suburbs up.

And they were waking up.

- Kendrick's *Alright* became a protest chant
- J. Cole had white kids talking about credit scores
- Nipsey was teaching about ownership and equity

And then he got shot.

So the industry pivoted:
- Flood the streets with vibe-only artists
- Get rid of lyrics
- Keep the BPM high and the IQ low
- Make being dumb, numb, and iced out the standard

Why?

Because a hypnotized people don't organize.
They stream.

And here's the worst part:
It's sold as freedom.
As expression.
As *"let them have their fun."*

Meanwhile, the real freedom fighters are starving.

They're told:
- Their bars are too complicated
- Their content won't trend
- Their message is too heavy for the kids

No.
It's too dangerous for the agenda.

This isn't music.
This is sonic sedation.

A trance.
A trap.
Literally and metaphorically.

They give the non-threatening, nonsensical shit a platform
and bury the griots.
The prophets.
The intellectual insurgents.

They don't want bars.
They want cages.

Where creativity stays circular.
And nothing leaves the loop.

So the next time someone tells you:

> "It's just a vibe, bro"

Ask yourself:
- Who curated the vibe?
- And what isn't being said?

Because the **Cult of Retard Rap** didn't kill hip-hop. **It colonized it.**

Turned it from resistance into rhythm.
From truth into trend.

And now the beat goes on.
But the message?

Buried under auto-tune and apathy.

THE INDIE CULT

Indoctrination Phrase: *"You've probably never heard of them."*
Core Doctrine: *Obscurity equals credibility*
Truth Bomb: *In your quest to escape the mainstream cult, you accidentally joined a more annoying one.*

Remember back in the day how everyone wanted to be the first to hear a band?

- The opener mattered
- The venue mattered
- The date you first saw them—that shit was currency

Because if you heard them before they blew up, you weren't just a fan—
You were chosen.

You weren't there for the fame.
You were there for the art.
You were there for the music, man.
You were real.

That was the lie that started it all.

Let me say this loud and slow:

The more indie you are, the more in a cult you are.
And not just any cult—
The Cult of Anti-Cult.

In trying to escape the mainstream brainwash,
you became everything you swore you hated.

> *(Not to be confused with The Anti-Cult Organization—we torch the bullshit, we don't curate it.)*

This is the group that **worships "authenticity" like it's an endangered species.**

– The ones who think mainstream = corrupt
– The ones who fetishize struggle, lo-fi production, and unreleased demos because polish is for the uninitiated

They don't consume music.
They curate an identity.

- Every playlist is a manifesto
- Every song is a personality fragment
- Every *"you wouldn't get it"* is a power play

Because in this cult, your value is directly tied to **how early you arrived.**

You didn't just discover music.
You colonized it before Pitchfork got there.

And what happens when your favorite artist starts succeeding?
 - When more people find out?
 - When their show sells out before you buy tickets?

Oh, now they're ruined.
Now they're overproduced.
Now they're too known.

Because The Indie Cult doesn't actually love music.
It fetishizes obscurity.
It turns niche into superiority.

This is **anti-pop elitism with a tote bag.**
Subcultural gatekeeping dressed up as taste.

And it's exhausting.

They pride themselves on anti-commercialism,
but still line up to buy:

- Limited run vinyls
- Hand-stitched band patches
- Cassette re-releases they'll never open

They're **capitalists in denial—**
buying "realness" at the merch table
while sneering at people in Target graphic tees.

They think liking something popular makes you shallow.
But liking something no one else knows about?

That's a personality trait.

They won't admit it, but every indie kid is just a failed cult leader in ironic shoes.

- They want exclusivity
- They want to own meaning
- They want to validate their isolation through taste

And that's the whole scam.

In trying to escape mass manipulation,
they became addicted to individualism.

- To being different
- To being the only one who "gets it"

> You're not more enlightened because you listen to bands with no vowels in their name.
> You're not more soulful because your favorite artist recorded their album in a shed with a haunted banjo.
> You're not immune to cults because you reject the mainstream.

You've just joined the counterculture chapter.

– Same emotional payoff
– Same psychological hijacking
– Just cooler font choices

The Indie Cult doesn't protect you from conformity.
It just sells you a version of it that's harder to critique.

Because how can it be a cult when it's handmade?
When it's underground?
When it's anti-everything?

I'll tell you how:

Because it makes you believe that your value lies in what no one else has heard yet.

And once they hear it?
You're obsolete.

The Indie Cult didn't save you from the system.
It just taught you to gatekeep your own joy.

THE CULT OF CANCEL

Indoctrination Phrase: *"We need to hold them accountable."*
Core Doctrine: *Morality is performative.*
Truth Bomb: *Opinions are like assholes—everybody's got one, and now they're monetizing them for clout.*

Welcome to the Cult of Cancel Culture,
where everyone is a public figure,
everything is evidence,
and every mistake is a sacrament—
offered up to the gods of outrage for digital penance.

This is the church of moral hyper-vigilance.
 – Where your past is never past
 – Where context is blasphemy
 – Where *"growth"* is performative, but **shame is permanent**

You fuck up publicly?
Off with your verified head.

You fuck up privately?
Screenshot. Caption. Viral.

This isn't justice.
This is ritualized punishment on a feed loop.
Retribution as content.
Twitter trials and Instagram inquisition—

from people who think *"accountability"* means
"I get to decide your fate based on a TikTok I saw 4 seconds ago."

And sure—some people deserve to get got.
Some people need a spotlight on their fuckery.

But cancel culture isn't about the transgression.
It's about the performance of reaction.

Because the currency here isn't truth.
It's **who can be louder, sooner, and more self-righteous than everyone else.**

You don't call people out anymore.
You call them down.

To the town square of the internet
for ritual humiliation.

And the people doing the calling?

Half of them are cosplaying justice.
The other half are **projecting their own shame in a safer direction.**

Because if we're burning someone else,
we don't have to look at ourselves.

We turned:
 – "I disagree with you" → **"You're dangerous."**
 – "I used to think like that too" → **"You're irredeemable."**
 – "That was 10 years ago" → **"Doesn't matter. Delete your platform."**

And for what?

To feel morally superior
in an economy of attention.

Because outrage is a drug.
 – It floods your brain
 – It validates your pain
 – It gives you a sense of agency
in a world that keeps fucking you

But the high wears off.
And someone has to pay.

So we find the next sacrifice:

– The next celebrity
– The next niche creator
– The next mutual who said something "problematic" in 2015
– The next person who got it wrong
in the wrong tone
at the wrong time

Because in this cult?

Silence is complicity.
But nuance? That shit is treason.

And don't get it twisted—this isn't about justice.

Justice allows for repair.
Justice has process.

This is:
 – Public spectacle
 – Algorithmic purging

And the worst part?

No one actually leaves.

You get "cancelled"
 → then you trend
 → then you rebrand
 → then you relaunch

Because cancellation isn't banishment.
It's a PR cycle.
It's entertainment.
A digital guillotine with affiliate links.

And meanwhile?

The people who are **actually dangerous**—
– Abusers
– Manipulators
– Predators

Slip through the chaos.

Because **outrage fatigue** made us care more about tone than trauma.

And the people you *could've* had a conversation with?

– Gone
– Fired
– Deleted
– Blocked into oblivion
with no chance to come back

Because we don't do restoration.
We do scorched earth.

All in the name of *"community standards"*
written by people who never left middle school emotionally.

This isn't community.
It's a purity cult with avatars.

So here's the truth:

Cancel culture doesn't hold power accountable. It devours anyone too messy, too human, or too slow to perform perfectly.

And the second you say:

> "Maybe there's more to this..."

You're next.

THE GAMER CHURCH

Indoctrination Phrase: *"It's just a game."*
Core Doctrine: *Skill equals worth. Emotion equals weakness.*
Truth Bomb: *You're not escaping reality. You're reenacting its worst parts—on repeat, with a headset.*

Welcome to **The Gamer Church**,
where fragile masculinity is baptized in Mountain Dew and the gospel is written in kill counts, leaderboards, and Reddit threads full of rage.

This is where boys go to feel powerful **without doing any of the work.**

It's not about fun.
It's about domination.
It's about control.
It's about feeling godlike in a space where:

- Failure has a respawn timer
- Accountability is mute

Every match?
A sermon.

Every *"noob"*?
A heretic.

Every woman who speaks in voice chat?
A threat to the hierarchy.

Because this isn't just play.
This is ritualized ego preservation.

The Gamer Church teaches you:

- Feelings = lag
- Inclusivity = cheating
- Women = distractions
- Losing = personal betrayal
- Therapy = weakness
- Rage = identity

And if you ever question it?

You'll be swarmed by the congregation.

Gatekeeping is holy.
Toxicity is tradition.
Casual players are to be **mocked, muted, and excommunicated.**

This cult doesn't welcome anyone.
It **surveils, tests, and humiliates** until you break—or submit.

Because only the "strongest" survive.
(**Translation:** only those who mimic the cult's rage rituals perfectly.)

The Gamer Church isn't just full of misogynists.
It manufactures them.
One kill cam at a time.

Because what better way to make someone feel like a man
than by handing him control, a weapon, and an audience—
without ever requiring him to evolve emotionally?

This is male fragility on steroids,
shoved into a console
and streamed for donations.

And make no mistake—
this cult feeds the next one.

THE INCEL CULT

Indoctrination Phrase: *"Women only want Chad."*
Core Doctrine: *Rejection is oppression*
Truth Bomb: *This isn't about love. It's about revenge for not being worshipped.*

The Incel Cult is what happens
when entitlement curdles into ideology.

They don't want partnership.
They want power over the people who don't want them.

They call it loneliness.
But it's control they're missing.

They call it being misunderstood.
But what they really mean is:
"Why won't women suffer for not choosing me?"

This is **male victimhood weaponized into violent theology.**
And it's fucking dangerous.

Because these aren't just sad, horny loners.
They're **radicalized rage-priests** who believe:

– Women owe them sex
– Feminism ruined the natural order
– The world was better when men dominated everything
– Emotional maturity is a scam
– Violence is justified when validation is denied

This isn't rejection—**it's insurrection.**
Disguised as dating commentary.
Masked as memes.
Funded by forums.
Groomed by algorithms.

And the worst part?
They think they're the oppressed ones.
That they're the resistance.
That hating women makes them brave.

They use pseudoscience to back up their bullshit.
They worship outdated gender roles
and turn "alpha" mythology into a religion.

And when they don't get what they want?

They fantasize about erasing the people who made them feel small.

- Elliot Rodger
- Alek Minassian
- Countless others whose names we never learn
until it's too late

Because this cult doesn't just isolate.
It radicalizes.

And here's the kicker:
Most of them started in The Gamer Church.

- In the Discords
- In the Twitch chats
- In the toxic little pockets

where jokes turned into dogma
where "it's just a game" became
"it's just women who are the problem."

The Incel Cult didn't come out of nowhere.
It was built.
Slowly.
Strategically.

By telling broken boys that their pain was someone else's fault.
That they weren't unlovable—
just too evolved for these dumb sluts.

And once that seed is planted?

It doesn't bloom.
It festers.

Until:

– Another woman dies
– Another group chat throws on a Pepe meme
– Another angry man convinces himself he's the victim of a system built to coddle women

Fuck these men.
Fuck their entitlement.
Fuck their delusions.
Fuck their community.
Fuck their fake logic.
Fuck their entire cult.

You're not oppressed.
You're just a coward with WiFi and a grudge.

THE SELFIE RELIGION

Indoctrination Phrase: *"If it's not on camera, did it even happen?"*
Core Doctrine: *Visibility is validation*
Truth Bomb: *You're not documenting your life. You're building a content shrine to your own algorithmic worth.*

Welcome to **The Selfie Religion**,
where the sacred trinity is:
 – Aesthetic
 – Affirmation
 – Audience

Worship begins with the front-facing camera.

This isn't self-expression.
This is digital worship.

Your god?
Yourself.
But only the curated version.
Only the filtered, posed, optimized, brand-aligned, emotionally-staged version of you.
You don't feel something until you post about it.

You don't cry without checking the lighting.
You don't even exist until it's documented.

What was once private reflection is now **performative vulnerability.**
What was once experience is now **content strategy.**

You aren't healing.
You're storyboarding your pain.

And you call it authenticity—
but every caption has been rewritten five times.
Every post approved internally by your own insecurity.
Every *"raw moment"* scheduled like a fucking product launch.

Because in this cult:
Nothing is real until it's been seen.

You don't ask *"How do I feel?"*
You ask:

> *"How will this land?"*

– Will it trend?
– Will it convert?
– Will it get validation in the form of metrics?

This isn't self-love.
It's self-surveillance.

Hyper-curated exhibitionism **disguised as self-acceptance.**

And let's be real:
It's not about memory.
It's about immortality.

About being seen and seen and seen and seen—
until the internet chokes on your presence.

- Your archive is your altar
- Your followers? Fellow disciples
- Your likes? Prayers answered
- Your trauma dump carousel post? A digital confession booth

And what do you pray for?
- Relevance
- Engagement
- A place in the feed

You're not asking to be known.
You're begging to not be forgotten.

Because in this religion, **disappearance is death.**
Go quiet for a week?
People start unfollowing your grief.

Log off too long?
You stop mattering.

But you're not addicted to attention.
You're afraid of erasure.
Because if you don't post it,
then who the fuck are you?

This cult trains you to:

- Look inward only to project outward
- Narrate your life in captions
- Treat every moment like a backdrop
- Evaluate your reflection through engagement analytics

Even your fucking shadow work has a thumbnail.

And don't even start with the *"It's for the memories"* crew.

Really?
Your memories needed a ring light and a discount code?

Your inner child didn't ask to be packaged into trauma content.
They asked to be held.
Not monetized.

But you'll call it empowerment.
Because that's the language of the cult.
It always is.

Make it sound like liberation
so no one questions how chained to the performance you've actually become.

The Selfie Religion doesn't want you to be yourself.
**It wants you to be an image.
An icon.
A living logo of your own identity crisis.**

– You don't reflect. You caption.
– You don't live. You frame.
– You don't heal. You perform your recovery for an audience of ghosts.

And the real shit?
They don't even care.

People aren't witnessing you.
They're scrolling past your soul like it's filler.

You're just part of the feed.
You thought you built a platform.
But what you really built was a prison.
One you update daily—
and call it authenticity.

THE CULT OF THE ALGORITHM

Indoctrination Phrase: *"It just knows me."*
Core Doctrine: *Choice is an illusion*
Truth Bomb: *You're not consuming content. You're being consumed by the code that curates you.*

Let's kill the fantasy:

You didn't pick that show.
You didn't choose that song.
You didn't fall down that TikTok rabbit hole.

You were pulled.

By an invisible god with no face, no name, and no morals—
but **more power over your psyche than your parents ever had.**

This is **The Cult of the Algorithm**,
where your tastes, beliefs, attention span, desires, and identity
**are engineered in real time by a formula no one understands—
but everyone obeys.**

Because let's be honest:

- You don't binge anymore
- You black out with intention
- You dissociate on schedule

You hand over your nervous system willingly—
because the machine has taught you
that **your exhaustion is entertainment's responsibility.**

The Algorithm doesn't care about what you love.
It cares about what keeps you scrolling.

It doesn't care if you're happy.
It cares if you engage.

It doesn't care if the content is true, healthy, or even human.
It cares how long your eyes stay open.

It's not feeding you content.
It's feeding off your patterns.

- Your rage clicks
- Your trauma loop
- Your 3am curiosity
- Your desperate search for dopamine
in a world that has no fucking joy left

And here's where it gets brutal:

It learns.

– Faster than you heal
– Smarter than you think
– More intimate with your subconscious than any therapist ever will be

You're not choosing anymore.
You're reacting to a curation of your own worst impulses.
Over and over and over again.

Because that docuseries you "discovered"?
That song you "randomly found"?
That hot take that "just happened to appear"?

That's not fate.
That's behavioral engineering.

You didn't stumble into it.
You were optimized into it.

And the more it knows you?
The less you know yourself.

Because you start mistaking personal resonance for digital accuracy.
You start believing:

- Your feed is truth
- Your content bubble is reality
- Your bias is insight
- Your triggers are taste

The Algorithm didn't just learn how to entertain you.
It learned how to program you.

- To silo you
- To use your pain to keep you compliant

Streaming platforms?
Just soft prisons with autoplay.

Social apps?
Digital Skinner boxes.

Music services?
Emotional clickbait generators dressed up as discovery.

And the more niche your feed feels?
The more you think it understands you?
The more fucked you are.

Because **it doesn't know you.**
It owns your input.
It replicates your insecurities.
It mirrors your anxiety.
It magnifies your echo chamber until it becomes your only voice.

And every time you think you're making a choice,

you're actually submitting to an invisible value system you never agreed to.

Because the algorithm isn't just feeding you content.
It's building your worldview.

- Quietly
- Completely
- Always for profit

You're not lost in the scroll.
You've been cultured into inertia.

And they'll call it *"personalized."*
They'll call it *"tailored."*
They'll call it *freedom of choice.*

But let's be honest:

**If your liberation has a "For You" tab—
you're not free.
You're just well-packaged obedience.**

THE CULT OF THE BIOPIC

Indoctrination Phrase: *"Their story needed to be told."*
Core Doctrine: *Trauma equals ticket sales*
Truth Bomb: *You didn't watch a tribute. You watched someone's deepest pain commodified, edited, and glamourized for award season.*

Let's get one thing straight:

Biopics aren't made to honor the truth.
They're made to **package it.**
Polish it.
Sell it.

And if that means warping history into a redemptive arc
with a swelling soundtrack and a tragic close-up?
So be it.

Because **truth doesn't win awards.
Narrative does.**

And that's what this cult feeds on:

✔ Add just enough pain to make it Oscar-worthy
✔ Remove just enough reality to keep it palatable
✔ Hire someone hot to play someone broken
✔ Blur every line until you can't tell what's real anymore

The Cult of the Biopic doesn't want nuance.
It wants emotional pornography.

It wants trauma you can consume in 128 minutes
and walk away from feeling *"moved,"*
without doing a single fucking thing about what caused it.

They take lives that were:

- Complex
- Radical
- Tragic
- Unmarketable

And **flatten them into cinematic digestibility.**

- Every rough edge filed down
- Every inconvenient truth omitted for pacing
- Every fucked-up system blurred into the background

While **individual suffering is center stage—**
dramatic, isolated, personal.

So when you leave the theater crying,
you're not mourning the system.
You're mourning the spectacle.

And here's the real manipulation:

They sell you the illusion that you now know this person.
That you've connected.
That you've done your empathy homework.

Nah.

You just binge-watched a human being's dismantling **with award-season cinematography.**

This isn't honoring their life.
It's mining it.

And the more marginalized the subject?
The more likely their **pain** is the plot.

- Not their ideas
- Not their resistance
- Not their joy
- Not their context

Just the suffering.
Just the addiction.
Just the betrayal.
Just the breakdown.

It's systemic voyeurism.
Sanitized just enough to make white liberals say *"important"*
without ever asking **who profited.**

They won't fund the actual people doing the work.
But they'll give millions to dramatize their downfall.
And then give trophies to actors pretending to survive it.

And if the person is still alive?

They'll interview them *just enough* for PR optics,
then ignore them when they say:

> "That's not what happened."

Because **accuracy isn't profitable.**
But a compelling trauma arc?
That's money.

This cult doesn't just rewrite stories.
It reconstructs memory.

So now:
What you watched becomes the truth.
And the truth becomes irrelevant.

Because **emotion wins.**
And emotion sells.
Especially when it's not yours.

So no, this isn't storytelling.
It's emotional colonialism.

– Your tears are their currency
– Your empathy is being harvested

You weren't honoring a legacy.
You were consuming a distortion.

And now you think you understand.
Which makes you less likely to question anything deeper.

That's the con.
That's the cult.

The Biopic didn't educate you.
It comforted you.

Wrapped injustice in aesthetics.
Gave you a narrative arc instead of a revolution.

So the next time someone says:

> "It's based on a true story…"

Ask them:

- **Whose version?**
- **Whose profit?**
- **Whose pain are you buying today?**

THE CULT OF NOSTALGIA

Indoctrination Phrase: *"Things were just better back then."*
Core Doctrine: *The past is safer than the truth*
Truth Bomb: *You didn't miss the good old days—you missed not knowing how fucked everything actually was.*

Let's not pretend.

Half of you bought this zine because the cover gave you a feeling.

- The cassette design
- The vintage fonts
- The grunge-era grit

It hit your dopamine like a mixtape from 1997, and you thought—
"This feels like something I used to love."

Yeah.
That's nostalgia.
That's the cult we're in right now.

> *(Not even subtle. You got played. It's okay. We all did.)*

Because the **Cult of Nostalgia** is the most seductive of them all.

It doesn't scream.
It soothes.
It doesn't demand.
It comforts.

It wraps your trauma in pop culture packaging
and sells it back to you as warmth.

And what does it tell you?

- That everything used to be simpler
- That you were happier when things were slower
- That the 90s were pure
- That childhood = safety
- That if we could just go back...

But **back to what, exactly?**

– To homophobia in sitcoms?
– To trauma in silence?
– To pre-diagnosed neurodivergence?
– To hidden abuse behind closed doors and VHS tapes?
– To parents who said "rub some dirt on it" instead of asking how you felt?

Yeah. That.

You don't miss the past.
You miss being numb.

You miss not knowing.
You miss believing in the illusion.
You miss not having words for what was hurting you.

Because once you wake up,
you can't unsee the architecture of the lie.

And nostalgia knows that.

So it doesn't try to argue.
It just plays your favorite song.
It just sends you a rerun.
It just shows you a filtered photo of a time that never really existed.

Because **Nostalgia** doesn't show you what was real.
It shows you what was survivable.

It edits out the dark parts.
It turns trauma into aesthetic.
And it makes you feel like longing is the same as truth.

It's not.
It's a coping mechanism.
It's emotional sepia tone.
And it's wildly profitable.

Just look around:

→ Reboots
→ Revivals
→ Legacy sequels
→ "Y2K" fashion from people born in 2006
→ Mental breakdowns disguised as Lisa Frank mood boards

It's not a vibe.
It's cultural escapism dressed up as identity.

Because when the present feels too broken,
and the future feels too scary,
the past becomes religion.

And that's the cult.

The **Cult of Nostalgia** tells you that the future can't be trusted.
So you anchor yourself to a manufactured memory.

And as long as you're looking back—
you're not asking what needs to change now.

But here's the redemption arc:
You found this.

Yes, you were pulled in by the feeling.
Yes, the cover made you remember something.
Yes, you were vulnerable to the exact thing this zine is eviscerating.

But that's the point.

We didn't design this to trick you.
We designed this to reveal what's been tricking you all along.

We're not here to shame you for playing into the cult.
We're here to help you break out of it.

– All of it
– The Pop Culture Poison
– The performance
– The programming
– The curated grief and commodified healing and identity-as-merch drop

This zine wasn't a trap.
It was a mirror.

And if you made it this far?
You see it now.

Welcome to The Anti-Cult Organization.
You don't have to be nostalgic anymore.
The future is calling.
And this time, you get to write it.

The Anti-Cult Organization was born as America entered its FAFO era.

We exist to expose the everyday cults you were taught to call normal—
and to arm you with the language to reject them.

This series isn't commentary.
It's deprogramming.

If you feel like something just cracked open,
good.
That was the point.

To see what we're building next, follow
@thanticultorg
or go to theanticult.org

www.ingramcontent.com/pod-product-compliance
Lightning Source LLC
Chambersburg PA
CBHW070641030426
42337CB00020B/4109